Cover illustrated by Tanya Kornikova
Illustrated by Michele Ackerman, Martha Avilés, Michelle Berg, Kate Kolososki, Margie Moore, Peggy Tagel, David Wojtowycz, and Maria Woods

Louis Weber, C.E.O.
Publications International, Ltd.
7373 North Cicero Avenue
Lincolnwood, Illinois 60712
Ground Floor, 59 Gloucester Place
London W1U 8JJ

Customer Service: 1-800-595-8484 or customer_service@pilbooks.com

www.pilbooks.com

8 7 6 5 4 3 2 1

Manufactured in China.

ISBN-13: 978-1-60553-748-1
ISBN-10: 1-60553-748-9

Welcome!

This Fun to Cut workbook has been specially designed to help prepare your child for school. You and your child should work together on each activity. In the front of the book, you will find simple, introductory exercises. As you work your way to the back of the book, the exercises will gradually become more complex and challenging.

Before you begin, show your child how to hold a pair of scissors properly. Your child's thumb should be placed in the top part of the handle. The pointer finger should wrap beneath the scissors. The middle finger should go in the bottom part of the handle. If there is enough room, the ring finger and little finger should stay in the handle next to the middle finger. As your child practices cutting this way, they will build important fine motor skills. As children gain fine motor skills, they build strength in the small

muscles in their hands. Activities that require fine motor skills, such as cutting and drawing, develop the accuracy and control children need in order to learn to write. Building these important skills helps prepare your child for school.

In addition to developing fine motor skills, the exercises in this book will challenge your child to distinguish shapes, practice counting, and follow simple directions. To make the most of each activity, keep these suggestions in mind:

- Tear out the page along the perforation and lay it flat on your work surface. This will help your child focus on just one activity at a time.

- Read the directions aloud.

- Let your child attempt each activity and only assist when necessary.

- Be positive and encouraging. Learning should be fun!

When you reach the end of the workbook, celebrate your child's accomplishments. Remove the certificate of achievement and help your child write their name on it so they can proudly display it.

Safety Guidelines:

1. Children should only use scissors under close supervision.

2. When you carry scissors, your hand should be wrapped around the blades with the blades pointing down.

3. To hand scissors to someone, keep your hand wrapped around the blades and point the handle toward the person.

4. When children carry scissors, remind them to walk slowly and watch where they are going.

Cut Straight Lines

Cut along the dotted lines.

Cut Zigzag Lines

Cut out the snakes.

Cut Wavy Lines

Cut out the jellyfish tentacles.

Let's build a sandwich!

Cut out the SQUARES for slices of bread.

Let's build a sandwich!

Cut out the CIRCLES for tomato slices.

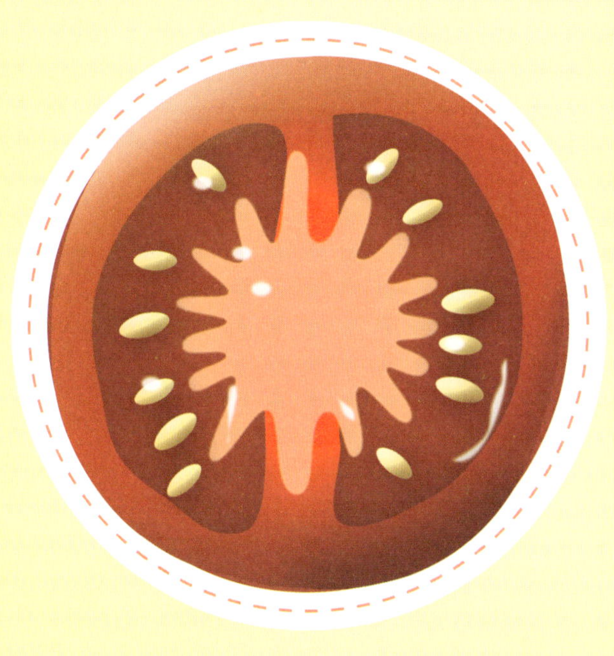

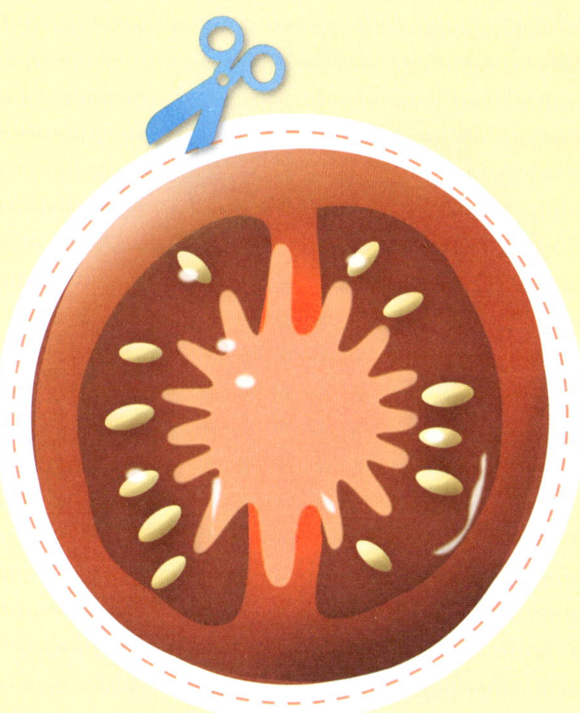

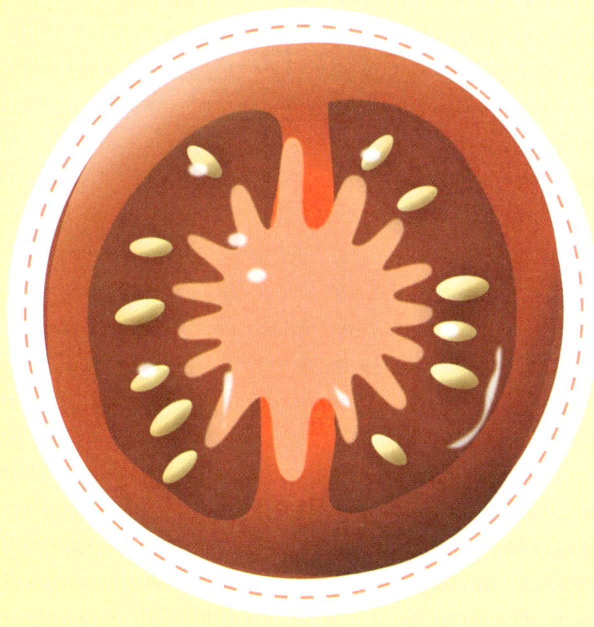

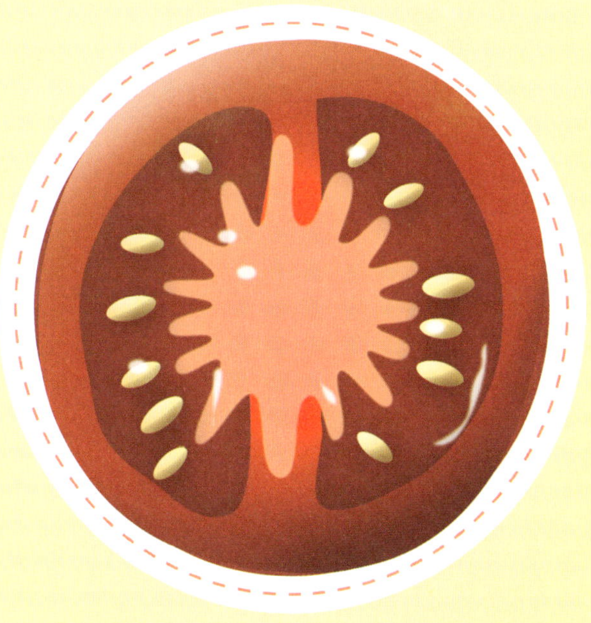

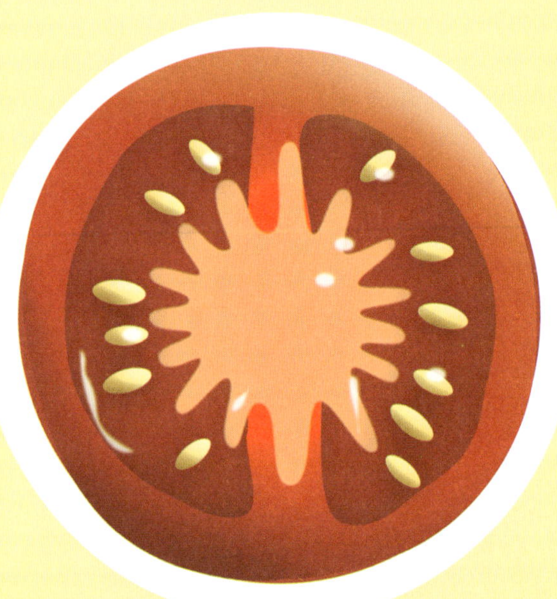
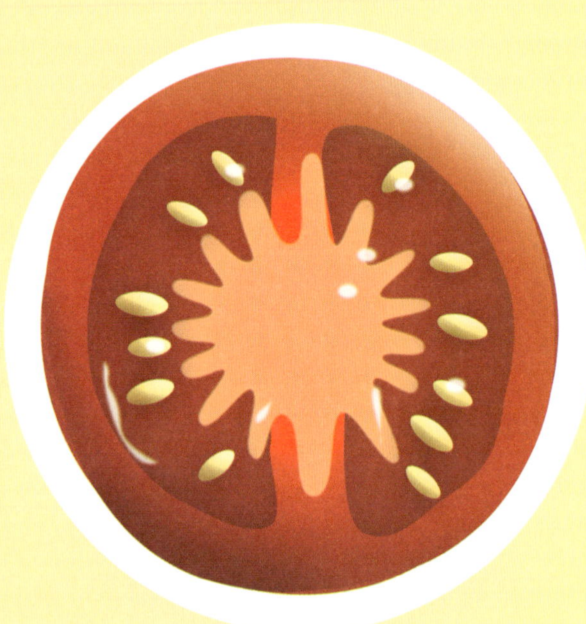
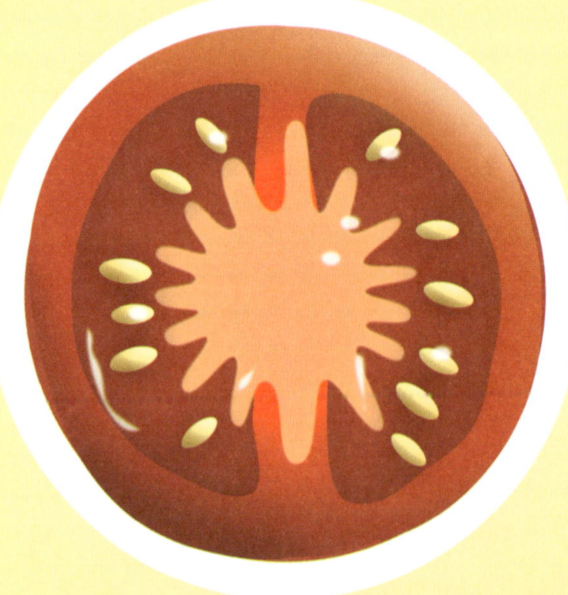
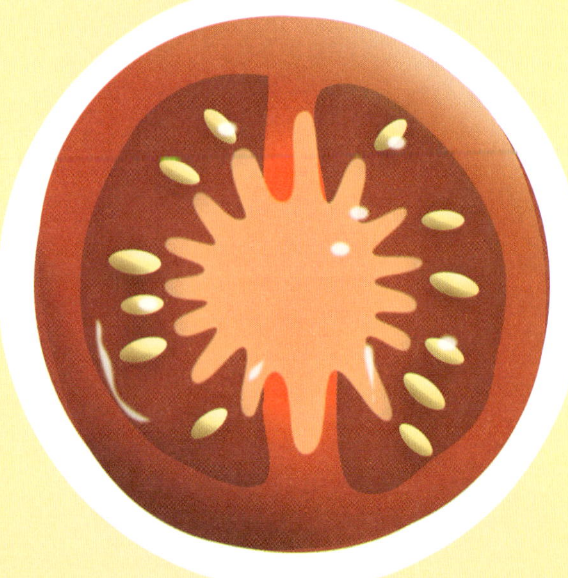

Let's build a sandwich!

Cut out the TRIANGLES for slices of cheese.

Let's build a sandwich!

Cut out the DIAMONDS for lettuce leaves.

Let's build a sandwich!

Cut out the RECTANGLES for bacon strips, and
cut out the OVALS for cucumber slices.

Let's have lunch!

Fruit salad, anyone? Cut out the placemat, and put your sandwich and fruit on the plate below.

Cut out 1 tree.
Cut out 2 kites.

Now glue or tape 1 tree and 2 kites into the scene above.

Glue or tape 3 flowers into the scene below.

Cut out 3 flowers.

Cut out 4 fish.

Now glue or tape 4 fish into the scene below.

Glue or tape 5 hats onto the 5 bears below.

Cut out 5 hats.

Play a Matching Game

Cut out the playing cards and lay them facedown. Each player flips over two cards at a time until all matches have been made.

Matching
Game
Matching
Game
Matching
Game
Matching
Game
Matching
Game
Matching
Game
Matching
Game
Matching
Game
Matching
Game
Matching
Game
Matching
Game
Matching
Game

Paper Chains

Use glue or tape to make loops out of the strips below, linking them together to make a paper chain.

Farm Puzzle

Cut out the puzzle pieces and arrange to create this scene.

Hula Puzzle

Cut out the puzzle pieces and arrange to create this scene.

Bird-Watching Puzzle

Cut out the puzzle pieces and arrange to create this scene.

Hey Diddle Diddle Puzzle

Cut out the puzzle pieces and arrange to create this scene.

Busy Bugs

Cut out these bugs and use them to play on the following scene pages.

Dinosaurs

Cut out these dinos and use them to play on the following scene pages.

On the Go

Cut out these vehicles and use them to play on the following scene pages.

On the Farm

Cut out these animals and use them to play on the following scene pages.

Make your own card!

Cut out the card and fold it in half.
Next, cut out the candles and glue some onto the cake.

fold here

Happy Birthday!

I hope the party
lasts all year!

Make your own card!

Cut around the outside of each card.
Next, fold each card in half.

fold here

May all your
wishes bloom!

Make your own card!

Cut out the card and fold it in half. Cut out the finger puppets, and ask an adult to cut out the finger holes.

fold here

It's your birthday...

...go bananas!

Make your own card!

Cut around the outside of each card.
Next, fold each card in half.

fold here

Gift Coupons

Cut out the coupons below and use them as gifts for your mom or dad.

This coupon is good for:

This coupon is good for:

This coupon is good for:

1
I LOVE
YOU
COUPON

1
I LOVE
YOU
COUPON

1
I LOVE
YOU
COUPON

1
I LOVE
YOU
COUPON

1
I LOVE
YOU
COUPON

1
I LOVE
YOU
COUPON

1
I LOVE
YOU
COUPON

1
I LOVE
YOU
COUPON

Ice Cream Shop

Cut out the tasty ice cream bits below.

Now glue or tape the ice cream treats here to build a cone that looks good enough to eat!

Cut out your cone creation from the front of this page and give it to a friend. Or, if you have leftover pieces, build another sundae below.

Funny Faces

Cut out these funny features to create your own characters on the following pages.

Now glue or tape the features onto the blank face above.
You can even add some silly scribbles of your own!

Dazzling Daisies

Cut out these petals and put the two pieces on top of each other so the petals are alternating. Attach the leaf behind. Then fold the bottom piece's petals forward.

Challenge Yourself

Cut along the butterfly's path and the snail's spiral shell.

Make a Flake

Did you know that no two snowflakes are exactly alike?
Cut a special snowflake designed by you!

1. Fold in half.
2.
3.
4.
5.
6.

Certificate of Achievement
I can CUT!
Congratulations!
(name)
has successfully completed the FUN TO CUT workbook.
Presented on
Presented by

Certificate of Achievement
I learned a lot!
I practiced cutting on paths.
I cut out shapes and characters.
I cut and assembled puzzles.
I made cards.
I followed directions.
I can cut anything!